perfect wedding favours

perfect wedding favours

Delectable homemade gifts for your wedding guests

Susannah Blake

photography by Carolyn Barber

392.5

LONDON · NEW YORK

Senior Designer Sonya Nathoo
Editor Rebecca Woods
Production Laura Grundy
Art Director Leslie Harrington
Editorial Director Julia Charles

Prop Stylist Liz Belton
Food Stylists Bridget Sargeson
and Jack Sargeson
Indexer Hilary Bird

First published in 2012 by
Ryland Peters & Small
20–21 Jockey's Fields
London WC1R 4BW

Text © Susannah Blake 2012
Design and photographs © Ryland
Peters & Small 2012

Printed in China

10 9 8 7 6 5 4 3 2 1

ISBN: 978-1-84975-253-4

A CIP record for this book is available from
the British Library.

Notes
• All spoon measurements are level,
unless otherwise specified.
• Eggs are medium unless otherwise
specified. Uncooked or partially cooked
eggs should not be served to the very old,
frail, young children, pregnant women or
those with compromised immune systems.
• When a recipe calls for the grated zest
of citrus fruit, buy unwaxed fruit and wash
well before using. If you can find only
treated fruit, scrub well in warm soapy
water before using.
• To sterilize preserving jars and bottles,
wash them in hot, soapy water and rinse
in boiling water. Place in a large saucepan
and cover with hot water. With the pan lid
on, bring the water to the boil and continue
to boil for 15 minutes. Turn off the heat and
leave the jars or bottles in the hot water
until just before they are to be filled. Invert
the jars or bottles on a clean tea towel
to dry. Sterilize the lids for 5 minutes by
boiling, or according to the manufacturer's
instructions. Jars and bottles should be
filled and sealed while they are still hot.

contents

introduction

The tradition of a small gift from the bride and groom to wedding guests dates back centuries to the European aristocracy, when small, elaborate boxes containing sugar cubes or confections were given to guests. As time passed and sugar became a less valuable commodity, the tradition became more widespread and sugared almonds became the favour of choice for centuries. A classic wedding favour, even at modern weddings, is still five sugared almonds tied up in beautiful fabric, with each of the five almonds representing health, wealth, happiness, fertility and longevity.

Today, wedding favours have become an intrinsic part of a wedding reception and can range from the simplest almonds or individual chocolate in a pretty gift box to more elaborate gifts personalized with the couple's names and wedding date. Whatever you choose though, presentation is always of the utmost importance, tying in with the theme of your wedding and the personalities of the bride and groom.

Even with all the planning in the world, the run-up to a wedding day can be fraught with last-minute panics and stresses. To avoid adding to those potential worries, make sure you're on top of the favour situation well ahead of time. Most of the recipes in this book need to be made just a few days before the wedding to ensure they are enjoyed at their very best. But you can avoid any nasty last-minute surprises by picking your chosen favour well ahead. At least a month before the wedding, have a trial run at making the recipe. Does it look and taste just as you want it to? Can you imagine making several batches without wanting to tear your hair out or sit down and weep in a corner? Give yourself plenty of time to order the perfect packaging. And if you're making the packaging from scratch, such as popcorn cones or little cellophane bags or crackers, I would recommend you make those well in advance.

With a little bit of planning, you can ensure that you have no nasty surprises when it comes to making your wedding favours and can simply enjoy relaxing and packaging up your favours the day before with family and friends.

candies & confectionery

turkish delight

Glistening cubes of pale pink Turkish delight, delicately scented with rosewater, make a delightfully romantic wedding favour. To serve at the table, place each piece of Turkish delight on a fresh rose petal arranged on a serving dish. Alternatively, a few cubes placed in a gift box tied up with ribbon, perhaps with a few dried rose petals, looks equally pretty.

Put 400 ml water in a large saucepan set over a low heat and add the rosewater and a little food colouring to make a vibrant pink. Sprinkle over the gelatine and sugar and heat gently, stirring occasionally, until the sugar has dissolved. Bring to the boil, then reduce the heat and simmer gently for 20 minutes.

When the mixture is ready, remove the pan from the heat and leave to cool for a couple of minutes. Skim off any foam from the top of the mixture then pour it into the prepared tin. Cover with clingfilm and leave to set for 3 hours in the fridge.

When set, turn the Turkish delight out onto a chopping board and use a sharp knife to slice the square into 8 strips, then slice into 8 strips in the opposite direction to make 64 cubes. Combine the icing sugar and cornflour then sift onto a large plate. Toss each cube of Turkish delight in the icing sugar mixture to coat.

Store the Turkish delight in an airtight container, layered between sheets of baking paper, until required. These can be made up to a week in advance.

2 tablespoons rosewater

pink food colouring

4 tablespoons gelatine powder

700 g caster sugar

2 tablespoons icing sugar

1 tablespoon cornflour

a 20-cm square cake tin, greased

makes 64

violet and rose chocolate shards

200 g dark chocolate,
broken into chunks

crystallized rose and
violet petals, to decorate

*a baking tray, lined with
non-stick baking paper*

makes about 50

These simple, spiky chocolate pieces, studded with sugary crystallized violet and rose petals, look so pretty arranged in a shallow dish or bowl. Create your own chocolate sculpture on the table by piling them up high in interesting shapes. Don't forget that chocolate melts very easily, so if you are having a summer wedding during blazingly hot weather, be sure to keep your chocolate shards cool.

Put the chocolate in a heatproof bowl set over a pan of barely simmering water. Leave the chocolate to stand until partially melted, then remove from the heat and stir until fully melted.

Pour the melted chocolate into the centre of the prepared baking tray and gently spread out to about 3 mm thick. Sprinkle crystalized violet petals over half of the chocolate and crystallized rose petals over the other half, spacing them well apart.

Leave the chocolate to set at cool room temperature. When set but not hard, remove the chocolate slab from the baking tray and use a sharp knife to slice it into long, delicate shards. You will end up with rose shards, violet shards and probably some plain or mixed shards.

When the chocolate is completely hard, gently peel off the baking paper and store in an airtight container in the fridge until required. These can be made up to a week in advance.

vanilla-blueberry fudge

500 g caster sugar
200 ml double cream
60 g butter
1 teaspoon vanilla extract
85 g dried blueberries

*a 20-cm square cake
tin, greased*

makes 64

Fudge is a wonderfully simple pleasure that everyone loves. There's something a little bit childish and nostalgic about it – so why not look out for small jars in which to pile your fudge, like old-fashioned candy jars, then top them with pretty fabric and a sprig of leaves or flowers.

Put the sugar, cream and butter in a large saucepan and heat very gently, stirring occasionally until the butter has melted and the sugar dissolved. Bring the mixture to the boil, without stirring, and continue to heat gently until the mixture reaches 118°C (240°F). (If you don't have a sugar thermometer, drop a little of the syrup into a glass of chilled water. It should keep it's shape and form a soft, flexible ball.)

When the syrup is ready, take the saucepan off the heat and stir in the vanilla extract. Beat the mixture until it thickens, then stir in the blueberries. Tip the mixture into the prepared cake tin and spread it evenly, smoothing down with a palette knife. Leave to cool completely.

When cooled and set, turn the fudge out onto a chopping board and use a sharp knife to slice the square into 8 strips, then slice into 8 strips in the opposite direction to make 64 cubes. Store in an airtight container until required. These can be made up to a week in advance.

coconut ice

397-g tin condensed milk
350 g unsweetened
desiccated coconut
375 g icing sugar, sifted
pink food colouring

*a 20-cm square cake
tin, greased*

makes 64

There's something wonderfully nostalgic about coconut ice and it can
bring a deliciously kitsch and slightly cheeky feel to a wedding breakfast.
Traditionally, coconut ice is pink and white striped and will look gorgeous
piled up on little glass cake stands decorated with ribbon.

Put the condensed milk, coconut and icing sugar in a large mixing bowl and stir well
to combine. It will make a very stiff mixture so will require a bit of work.

Spoon half of the mixture into the prepared cake tin and spread out in an even layer,
pressing down well with the back of a spoon.

Add a few drops of pink food colouring to the remaining mixture and stir well to
combine, adding more food colouring if necessary to achieve the desired shade.
Spoon the pink mixture on top of the white and spread out evenly, pressing down
well with the back of a spoon. Cover with clingfilm and leave to set overnight.

Turn the coconut ice out onto a chopping board and use a sharp knife to slice
the square into 8 strips, then slice into 8 strips in the opposite direction to make
64 cubes. Store in an airtight container until required. These can be made up to
a week in advance.

honeycomb shards

85 g unsalted butter
85 g golden syrup
150 g caster sugar
2 teaspoons bicarbonate
of soda

*a baking tray, greased
with flavourless oil*

makes about 40

Melt-in-the-mouth honeycomb toffee is delicious served plain or drizzled with dark chocolate. Present shards of honeycomb in pretty gift boxes that match the colour scheme of the wedding, or, for a simple, old-fashioned feel, you could package it in brown paper bags lined with pretty pastel-coloured tissue paper.

Put the butter, golden syrup and sugar in a large saucepan and heat gently until melted and the sugar has dissolved. Bring to the boil for about 6 minutes, without stirring. Swirl the pan occasionally to achieve an even colour, until the mixture is golden brown.

Remove the pan from the heat, quickly stir in the bicarbonate of soda – being very careful as the mixture will bubble and expand rapidly – and immediately pour into the prepared baking tray. Leave to cool and set completely, then break into shards.

Store the honeycomb in an airtight container until required.These can be made up to a week in advance.

fresh strawberry marshmallows

125 g strawberries, hulled
1 teaspoon lemon juice
2½ tablespoons gelatine powder
450 g caster sugar
160 ml golden syrup
4–5 tablespoons cornflour, for dusting

a 22 x 24-cm baking tin, lined with clingfilm and greased
a sheet of clingfilm large enough to cover the tin, greased
a smaller, round cookie cutter (optional)

makes about 130

Homemade marshmallows made with fresh strawberries make a lovely gift packaged in clear cellophane bags and tied with ribbon or ricrac. For an extra special touch, slip a sachet of luxury hot chocolate into the bag so your guests can enjoy an indulgent treat when they arrive home after the wedding.

Put the strawberries in a food processor and blend to a smooth purée. Pour into a large mixing bowl and stir in the lemon juice. Sprinkle over the gelatine powder and leave to soak.

Put the sugar, syrup and 200 ml water in a saucepan and heat very gently, stirring occasionally, until the sugar has completely dissolved. Bring to the boil and heat to 140°C (275°F), then remove from the heat and leave to cool for a couple of minutes.

Using an electric hand whisk on high speed, whisk the strawberry mixture until well blended. Reduce the speed to medium, then gradually drizzle the syrup down the edge of the mixing bowl, whisking all the time. Whisk for about 10 minutes until the mixture is very thick and throwing out strands from the beaters.

Pour the mixture into the lined baking tin and lay the sheet of greased clingfilm over the top. Leave to set in a cool place for at least 2 hours until the marshmallow feels firm and set.

Peel off the clingfilm and lightly dust the top of the marshmallow with about 1 tablespoon cornflour. Turn out onto a board and peel off the remaining clingfilm. Dust with more cornflour, then cut into 2-cm cubes using a sharp, greased knife (the cubes will be very sticky so handle with care). Alternatively, cut rounds from the marshmallow using a small cookie cutter (you will end up with fewer marshmallows). Sift the remaining cornflour onto a large plate and roll each marshmallow to coat. Toss well to remove any excess cornflour.

Store the marshmallows in an airtight container until required. These can be made up to a week in advance.

white chocolate cake pops

2 tablespoons double cream

25 g butter

100 g white chocolate, broken into chunks

175 g plain sponge cake, such as Madeira cake, finely crumbled

To decorate

200 g white chocolate, broken into chunks

pink heart sugar sprinkles

20 lollipop sticks

makes 20

These cuter-than-cute cake pops will make your guests smile as they sit down to enjoy the wedding feast. With a fudgy centre and crisp white chocolate coating they are delicious and easy to make. Decorating them can be a great activity for the bride and her hens – possibly using a glass of champagne or two to channel their creative flair!

Put the cream, butter and 100 g white chocolate in a heatproof bowl set over a pan of barely simmering water. Leave to stand until melted, then remove from the heat and stir in the cake crumbs. Chill in the fridge for about 1 hour, until firm.

Take heaped teaspoonfuls of the mixture and roll into balls roughly the size of a small walnut. Gently insert a lollipop stick into each one, then leave to chill and set overnight.

To decorate, melt the 200 g white chocolate in a heatproof bowl set over a pan of barely simmering water. Remove from the heat and leave to cool. Dip the cake pops in the chocolate, turning to coat, then decorate with the heart sugar sprinkles. Leave to set, then chill. (Shot glasses make a good place to stand your pops while they set.)

Store the cakepops in an airtight container until required. These can be made up to a week in advance.

golden dark chocolate truffles

250 g dark chocolate,
broken into chunks
250 ml double cream
50 g butter, diced
edible gold leaf,
for decorating

a melon baller
a baking tray, lined with
non-stick baking paper
a soft brush
petits fours cases

makes about 40

Rich, buttery truffles make wonderful petits fours for a wedding, but coating them in a thin layer of edible gold leaf makes them even more special. Edible gold leaf is available over the internet and from cake decorating shops. It is supplied in thin sheets, interleaved with tissue paper. Look for tiny gift boxes and nestle a truffle inside each one. You may want to make your truffles slightly larger depending on the size of your chosen box.

Put the chocolate in a food processor and blitz until finely chopped, then transfer to a mixing bowl.

In a small saucepan, gently heat the cream and butter together until almost boiling, then pour over the chocolate in the mixing bowl and stir until smooth. Cover and chill in the fridge for about 4 hours, until the mixture is firm.

Scoop up rounds of the mixture using a melon baller, then gently roll into balls and place on the prepared baking tray.

Chill again for about 1 hour, then gently roll the top half of each truffle on a sheet of gold leaf and press to the surface using the brush. Place each truffle in a petit four case and store in an airtight container in the fridge until required. These can be made up to a week in advance.

cakes & bakes

bite-sized brownie squares

60 g butter

125 g dark chocolate, broken into chunks

125 g caster sugar

2 eggs

60 g plain flour

a 20-cm square cake tin, lined with non-stick baking paper

makes 36

Everyone loves rich, chocolatey brownies, so stack up these bite-sized ones and bind with a strip of baking paper, finishing with a ribbon and a small posy of silk flowers. If you like your brownies nutty, throw a handful of walnut pieces into the mix when you add the flour.

Preheat the oven to 180ºC (350ºF) Gas 4.

Put the butter and chocolate chunks in a heatproof bowl and heat gently over a pan of barely simmering water until melted. Remove from the heat and leave to cool for about 5 minutes. Stir in the sugar, then beat in the eggs. Sift over the flour and fold in.

Pour the mixture into the prepared cake tin and bake in the preheated oven for about 17 minutes, until firm to the touch and pale on top. Leave to cool in the tin.

Turn the brownie out onto a chopping board and use a sharp knife to slice the square into 6 strips, then slice into 6 strips in the opposite direction to make 36 cubes.

Store the brownies in an airtight container until required. These can be made up to 4 days in advance.

floral baby cake bites

115 g butter

115 g caster sugar

2 eggs

½ teaspoon vanilla extract

115 g self-raising flour

2 tablespoons raspberry jam

To decorate

600 g icing sugar

1 tablespoon golden syrup

½ teaspoon vanilla extract

blue, yellow and pink food colouring

ready-made sugar flowers

2 x 20-cm square cake tins, greased and lined with non-stick baking paper

petits fours cases

makes 49

These pretty bite-sized cakes make wonderful petits fours and look lovely arranged in paper cases on elegant cake stands on the tables. Use ready-made sugar flower decorations, which look professional and make your life a lot simpler! Most cake decorating shops and online stockists have a beautiful selection to choose from.

Preheat the oven to 180°C (350°F) Gas 4.

In a large mixing bowl, beat together the butter and sugar until pale and creamy. Beat in the eggs one at a time, then stir in the vanilla extract. Sift the flour over the mixture, then fold everything together.

Divide the mixture between the prepared cake tins and bake in the preheated oven for about 13 minutes, until risen and the top springs back when gently pressed with a fingertip. Turn out onto a wire rack to cool.

When cooled, spread a thin layer of jam over one cake and place the second cake on top, patting down. Using a sharp knife, gently slice the cake into 7 strips, then slice into 7 strips in the opposite direction to make 49 cubes. Arrange the cubes on a wire rack, spacing well apart.

Put the icing sugar, golden syrup, vanilla extract and 4½ tablespoons water in a bowl and stir to combine. Divide the mixture between three heatproof bowls and tint each a different colour. Place one bowl over a pan of barely simmering water, stirring, for 3 minutes. If the icing remains very thick, add a drop of water at a time until you achieve a pouring consistency. Working quickly, spoon the icing over one-third of the cakes and top each with a sugar flower whilst still sticky. (If the icing becomes hard, return to the heat briefly until thinned.) Repeat with the remaining icing and cake cubes, returning each to the wire rack to set. When the icing is dry, place each cake in a petit four case.

Store the cake bites in an airtight container until required. The cake can be made a few days in advance, but it is best to leave the decorating until the day before the wedding.

mini cupcakes

115 g butter, at room temperature

115 g caster sugar

grated zest of 1 lemon

2 eggs

115 g self-raising flour

To decorate

175 g unsalted butter, at room temperature

450 g icing sugar, sifted

3 tablespoons freshly squeezed lemon juice

food colouring in your choice of colours

sugar sprinkles

silver dragées

a 24-hole mini muffin tin, lined with paper cases

a piping bag fitted with a large star nozzle

makes 24

Baby cupcakes with a swirl of pretty pastel icing and packaged in decorative boxes make a lovely gift for your guests, either to eat at the wedding or to take home and enjoy later. Look online for boxes to package your cakes in. To accommodate a pair of cupcakes you will need a box measuring approximately 10 cm x 5 cm x 7 cm high.

Preheat the oven to 180ºC (350ºF) Gas 4.

In a large mixing bowl, beat together the butter and sugar until pale and creamy. Beat in the lemon zest and then the eggs, one at a time. Sift the flour over the mixture, then fold everything together.

Spoon the cake mixture into the paper cases and bake in the preheated oven for about 15 minutes, until risen and golden and the sponge bounces back when gently pressed with a fingertip. Transfer the cakes to a wire rack and set aside to cool.

To decorate, beat together the butter, icing sugar and lemon juice with an electric hand whisk until smooth and creamy. Tint with the food colouring of your choice (or divide into two batches and tint two different colours) and briefly beat again to achieve an even colour. Spoon the icing into the piping bag and pipe a swirl on top of each of the cupcakes. (Repeat with the second batch of icing, if using two colours.) Scatter with sugar sprinkles and finish with a silver dragée.

Store the cupcakes in an airtight container until required. The cupcakes can be made a few days in advance, but it is best to leave the decorating until the day before the wedding.

jewelled florentines

Sweet, melt-in-the-mouth florentines are the classic petit four and have a natural place in the list of edible wedding favours. These ones are coated in a thin layer of white chocolate, but they are delicious made with dark or milk chocolate, too. Arrange them on a decorative plate on the table or package up little stacks of florentines in delicate netting, tied with ribbon.

50 g unsalted butter

50 g caster sugar

3 tablespoons double cream

25 g flaked almonds

50 g pistachio nuts, chopped

25 g walnuts, chopped

60 g mixed glacé fruits, such as apricots, cherries, citrus peel and angelica

2 tablespoons plain flour

100 g white chocolate, broken into chunks, to decorate

2 baking trays, lined with non-stick baking paper and greased

makes 24

Preheat the oven to 180°C (350°F) Gas 4.

Put the butter, sugar and cream in a large saucepan and heat very gently until the butter has melted. Bring to the boil, then remove from the heat and stir in the nuts, glacé fruits and flour.

Drop teaspoonfuls of the mixture onto the prepared baking trays, spacing well apart. Bake in the preheated oven for about 10 minutes until golden. Remove from the oven and, whilst still warm, tidy the edges of each florentine by using a knife to press around the edge of each one to make neat rounds, then leave to cool for about 10 minutes. Carefully peel off the baking paper then transfer to a wire rack to cool completely.

Melt the chocolate in a heatproof bowl set over a pan of barely simmering water. Use a palette knife to spread the base of each florentine with a thin layer of melted chocolate. Leave to firm up slightly, then make a wavy pattern in the chocolate using the tines of a fork before leaving to set completely.

Store the florentines in an airtight container until required. These can be made up to 3 days in advance.

meringue kisses

2 egg whites
115 g caster sugar

a piping bag fitted with a large round nozzle
2 baking trays, lined with non-stick baking paper

makes about 50

There's something utterly irresistible about fluffy white meringues. They look lovely tucked into boxes and tied with ribbon, or equally good piled up on cake stands and scattered with pale pink rose petals. If you're feeling more adventurous, you could even string them into garlands with dried rosebuds or petals to decorate the tables or venue. If you're arranging your meringues as a centrepiece or table decoration, serve with a little dish of clotted cream and fresh strawberries, too, for guests to dunk.

Preheat the oven to 110ºC (225ºF) Gas ¼.

In a spotlessly clean, grease-free bowl, whisk the egg whites with an electric hand whisk until they stand in stiff peaks. Gradually add the sugar, a spoonful at a time, whisking thoroughly between each addition until the mixture is thick and glossy.

Spoon the meringue into the piping bag and pipe swirls onto the prepared baking trays. Bake in the preheated oven for 1 hour until crisp and dry. Remove from the oven and leave to cool.

Store the meringue kisses in an airtight container until required. These can be made up to 4 days in advance.

celebration cookies

blossom cookies

85 g butter, at room
temperature
100 g caster sugar
1 egg yolk
200 g plain flour
2 large egg whites
500 g icing sugar, sifted
leaf green food colouring
lemon juice, for drizzling
ready-made sugar flowers
or 200 g pink ready-to-roll
fondant icing*

*a 7-cm square cookie
cutter (optional)*
2 baking trays, greased
*2 piping bags fitted with
small round nozzles*
*a blossom plunger cutter
(optional)*

makes 10

These cookies have a lovely glossy, smooth icing but despite their professional appearance they are deceptively simple to make. Choose any colour of flower you like to match your wedding theme. Pretty pastels look good against the green stems.

In a large mixing bowl, cream together the butter and sugar, then beat in the egg yolk. Sift the flour over the mixture and stir well to combine. Press the dough into a ball, wrap in cling film and chill for about 1 hour.

Preheat the oven to 180ºC (350ºF) Gas 4. Roll out the dough on a lightly floured surface to about 6 mm thick and cut into 7-cm squares using a knife or cookie cutter. Place the squares on the prepared baking trays and bake in the preheated oven for about 14 minutes until just colouring at the edges. Transfer to a wire rack to cool.

Beat the egg whites and icing sugar together to make a thick, smooth icing suitable for piping. Spoon one-quarter of the mixture into a separate bowl and tint green with the food colouring, then press a layer of clingfilm over the surface to keep it fresh.

Spoon about one-third of the white icing into a piping bag and pipe a border around the cookies about 5 mm from the edge. Add a little lemon juice to the remaining icing in the bowl and stir to make a good drizzling consistency (similar to double cream). Drizzle the thinner icing inside the boundary lines to fill, then set aside to firm.

Spoon the reserved green icing into the second piping bag and pipe delicate stems across the cookies. Using a small blob of icing on the back of each flower, attach the sugar flowers to the stems and leave to set. When set, store the cookies in an airtight container until required. The cookies can be made up to 4 days in advance, but it is best to leave the decorating until only 1 or 2 days before the wedding.

*You can buy ready-made sugar flowers from cake-decorating shops, but they are very easy to make yourself using ready-to-roll fondant icing. Break off a chunk of icing and roll it out on a surface lightly dusted with icing sugar. Cut out blossoms using a small blossom cutter. Using a palette knife, gently lift the flowers onto a curved flower former. Leave to dry completely before using to decorate your cookies. You can make the flowers several weeks in advance and store in an airtight container until required.

ribboned sugar cookies

These simple buttery cookies look pretty mixed and matched. Choose the colour of the ribbon to match the colour scheme of your wedding.

115 g butter, at room temperature

50 g caster sugar, plus extra for sprinkling

1 egg yolk

175 g plain flour

2 tablespoons milk, to glaze

To decorate

200 g ready-to-roll fondant icing

2 tablespoons apricot jam, sieved

edible gold lustre

a 7.5-cm heart cookie cutter

2 baking trays, greased

a drinking straw

a soft-bristled brush

14 lengths of organza ribbon

makes 14

In a large mixing bowl, cream together the butter and sugar, then beat in the egg yolk. Sift the flour over the mixture and stir well to combine. Tip the mixture out onto a lightly floured surface and knead gently to make a soft dough. Wrap in clingfilm and chill for 30 minutes.

Preheat the oven to 180°C (350°F) Gas 4. Roll out the dough on a lightly floured surface to about 6 mm thick. Stamp out hearts using the cutter and arrange on the prepared baking trays. If making simple sugar-sprinkled cookies, use a pastry brush to lightly glaze the top of each cookie with milk and then sprinkle them generously with sugar, otherwise, leave them bare. Make a hole at the top of each cookie with the straw, then bake the cookies in the preheated oven for about 10 minutes or until pale golden. Leave to cool on the baking trays for a few minutes then transfer to a wire rack to cool completely.

For the iced cookies, roll out the fondant icing to 2 mm thick on a sheet of baking paper. Brush a thin layer of apricot jam over the cookies. With the cutter, stamp out hearts from the icing and use to top each of the cookies. Using the straw, make a hole in the icing above the original cookie hole. Using a soft-bristled brush, dust the cookies with gold lustre and leave to dry. You can achieve different effects by brushing on varying amounts of the lustre, or could even leave some plain white.

Store the cookies in an airtight container until required. These can be made up to 3 days in advance. Thread each cookie with organza ribbon and tie in a bow.

confetti cookies

These cute cookies look adorable scattered over the tables. Frost them in your wedding colours or decorate them in pastel colours just like old-fashioned paper confetti. Look out for sets of mini cookie cutters in classic confetti shapes such as hearts, blossom, horseshoes and clover.

150 g plain flour
100 g butter, chilled and diced
85 g caster sugar
1 egg yolk

To decorate
200 g icing sugar
2 tablespoons lemon juice

food colouring (pastel lilacs, blues, greens, pinks and yellows all work well)

mini heart, horseshoe and flower cookie cutters (about 2.5 cm across)

2 baking trays, greased

makes about 80

Put the flour and butter in a food processor and blitz until the mixture resembles fine breadcrumbs. Add the sugar and egg yolk and blitz until the mixture starts to come together. Turn out onto a lightly floured surface and knead until it forms a dough. Press into a ball, wrap in clingfilm and chill for at least 30 minutes.

Preheat the oven to 180°C (350°F) Gas 4. Roll out the cookie dough on a lightly floured surface to about 5 mm thick, then stamp out shapes using the cutters. Arrange on the baking trays, then bake in the preheated oven for about 10 minutes until pale golden. Transfer to a wire rack to cool.

To decorate, sift the icing sugar into a bowl, then stir in the lemon juice to make a smooth, thick icing that drizzles off the spoon, adding a little more water if necessary. Divide into smaller bowls (according to how many colours you want to decorate your confetti) and tint each bowl of icing a different colour. Dip each cookie face down into a bowl of icing, allow the excess to drizzle off, then turn right-side up and leave to dry on the wire rack.

Store the cookies in an airtight container until required. The cookies can be made up to 4 days in advance, but it is best to leave the decorating until only 1 or 2 days before the wedding.

gingerbread loveheart napkin ties

115 g butter, at room temperature

115 g soft brown sugar

1 egg

75 g golden syrup

400 g plain flour

1 teaspoon ground ginger

75 g white chocolate, to decorate

a 6.5-cm heart cookie cutter

a drinking straw

2 baking trays, greased

a piping bag fitted with a small round nozzle

40 x 70-cm lengths 5-mm wide satin ribbon

makes about 40

Why bother with napkin rings when you can use these cute and delicious gingerbread cookies instead? They look just gorgeous and bring a fun twist to any wedding table. Decorate them simply or, if you are feeling creative, ice names on them and use them as a napkin ring, favour and place setting in one. Choose ribbon colours to complement your wedding colours and flowers.

In a large mixing bowl, beat together the butter and sugar until pale and creamy, then beat in the egg followed by the syrup. Sift the flour and ginger over the mixture and fold in. Turn out on to a lightly floured surface and knead gently to make a soft dough, then press into a ball, wrap in clingfilm and chill for 30 minutes.

Preheat the oven to 180°C (350°F) Gas 4.

Roll out the dough on a lightly floured surface to about 5 mm thick. Cut out hearts using the cookie cutter and make a hole for the ribbon at the top of each heart using a drinking straw.

Arrange the cookies on the baking trays and bake in the preheated oven for about 12 minutes until starting to colour around the edges. Leave to cool for a few minutes on the tray, then transfer to a wire rack to cool completely.

To decorate, break the white chocolate into a heatproof bowl set over a pan of barely simmering water. Stir until melted, then remove from the heat and leave to cool a little. Spoon the chocolate into the piping bag and pipe decorations, such as lines and dots or guests' names, on the cookies. Leave in a cool place to set.

Store the cookies in an airtight container until required. The cookies can be made up to 4 days in advance, but it is best to leave the decorating until only 1 or 2 days before the wedding.

To make the napkin ties, wrap the ribbon around the napkin, tying the cookies in place and secure with a knot, leaving the ends of the ribbon loose.

sparkling lovebird cookies

These simple sparkling sugar cookies look gorgeous nestled on your guests' folded napkins. They look good on both white or coloured linen. You could also try sprinkling on a little silver or transparent edible sparkle, too.

115 g butter, at room temperature

50 g caster sugar

1 egg

200 g plain flour

1 tablespoon ground almonds

To decorate

50 g icing sugar

2 teaspoons lemon juice

granulated sugar, for sprinkling

edible glitter or sprinkles (optional)

an 8-cm dove cookie cutter

2 baking trays, greased

makes about 24

In a large mixing bowl, beat together the butter and sugar until pale and creamy. Beat in the egg, then sift the flour and almonds over the mixture and fold in. Knead gently to make a soft dough, then press into a ball, wrap in clingfilm and chill for about 1 hour.

Preheat the oven to 180ºC (350ºF) Gas 4.

Roll out the dough on a lightly floured surface to about 4 mm thick and stamp out doves using the cookie cutter. Place the doves on the prepared baking trays and bake in the preheated oven for about 10 minutes, until the cookies are pale golden brown. Leave to cool for a couple of minutes on the tray, then transfer the cookies to a wire rack to cool completely.

To decorate, mix together the icing sugar and lemon juice until smooth. Brush a thin layer of the mixture over a cookie with a pastry brush and sprinkle generously with granulated sugar. Repeat with the remaining cookies. When dry, shake off the excess sugar and sprinkle over a small amount of edible glitter or some sprinkles, if using.

Store the cookies in an airtight container until required. These can be made up to 4 days in advance.

double chocolate name cookies

150 g butter, at room temperature

150 g caster sugar

2 egg yolks

50 g dark chocolate, melted

300 g plain flour

75 g white chocolate, to decorate

an 8.5-cm round, serrated cookie cutter

2 baking trays, greased

a piping bag fitted with a small round nozzle

makes 10

Getting your seating plan just right can be a stressful job, so inject some fun into it with these quirky name-card cookies. Go for the simple chocolate on chocolate approach or decorate with further embellishments such as gold or silver dragées. Tuck each cookie into a small envelope decorated with bows, flowers or butterflies for a lovely decorative finish, as well as an easy way for your guests to take them home to enjoy.

Preheat the oven to 180°C (350°F) Gas 4.

In a large mixing bowl, beat together the butter and sugar until pale and creamy. Beat in the egg yolks, followed by the melted dark chocolate. Sift the flour over the mixture and fold in. Turn out onto a lightly floured surface and knead gently to make a soft dough, then press into a ball, wrap in clingfilm and chill for about 30 minutes.

Roll out the dough between two sheets of baking paper to about 6 mm thick. Cut out rounds with the cutter and arrange on the prepared baking trays. Bake in the preheated oven for 10–12 minutes. Leave the cookies to cool on the trays for a few minutes, then, using a spatula, transfer the cookies to a wire rack to cool completely.

To decorate, break the white chocolate into a heatproof bowl set over a pan of barely simmering water. Stir until melted, then remove from the heat and leave to cool a little. Spoon the chocolate into the piping bag and pipe names in the centre of the cookies, then decorate around the names with lines, squiggles, dots and hearts. Leave in a cool place to set.

Store the cookies in an airtight container until required. The cookies can be made up to 4 days in advance, but it is best to leave the decorating until only 1 or 2 days before the wedding.

other treats

strawberry wedding preserve

Spread the love with beautifully presented jars of fruit conserve for your guests to take away. You can buy matching miniature jars, or create a more personal look using a mixture of different small jars, such as those used for spices, condiments, pastes and baby food. Finish the jars with pretty fabric or luxurious lace tied on with ribbon or coloured string and pretty hand-written tags. These are great favours if you are worried about time, as they can be made weeks or even a couple of months in advance.

1.25 kg strawberries, hulled

1.25 kg granulated sugar

freshly squeezed juice of 2 lemons

10 small sterilized jars (see page 4)

10 fabric circles with a design of your choosing

string or ribbon

makes about 10 small jars

Quarter the strawberries and put them in a large, non-metallic bowl. Sprinkle over the sugar and lemon juice, then cover with clingfilm and leave to stand overnight.

Tip the fruit mixture into a preserving pan and heat gently, stirring until the sugar has completely dissolved. Boil for 10–15 minutes to 105°C (220°F), skimming off any scum that rises to the surface. Leave to stand for 5 minutes, then stir. Carefully pour the preserve into the sterilized jars using a funnel, seal immediately then leave to cool.

Decorate your jars with rounds of fabric tied around the neck with a piece of string or ribbon. You could also add a hand-written gift tag for an extra-personal touch.

hazelnut and almond praline clusters

115 g granulated sugar
60 g hazelnuts
60 g flaked or split
blanched almonds

*a large baking tray,
greased*

makes about 8 packages

These golden, nutty caramel bites taste divine and look gorgeous wrapped up in simple cellophane packages tied simply with ribbon or decorated with other ornaments, such as these cute buttons. Break into small pieces and apportion several per package, or break off larger chunks and wrap individually.

Put the sugar in a large, heavy-based pan and heat gently over a low–medium heat, without stirring, until the sugar starts to melt. At this point, stir to mix thoroughly and continue to heat until clear and pale golden.

Add the hazelnuts and almonds to the pan, stir and cook for about 1 minute. Tip the caramel-coated nuts out onto the prepared baking tray, spreading out gently. Leave to cool for about 20 minutes before breaking into pieces.

If packaging immediately, make sure the nuts are completely cool first. Otherwise, store the praline clusters in an airtight container until required. These can be made up to a week in advance.

golden caramel popcorn

Sweet, sugary popcorn coated in golden drizzles of caramel look gorgeous piled into cones made from decorative paper. If the idea of making your own cones is too much, try piling the popcorn up into decorative paper cups or brightly coloured candy-striped bags.

1 tablespoon sunflower oil
100 g popcorn kernels
225 g granulated sugar
80 g golden syrup

2 baking trays, greased

makes about 12 bags

First prepare the popcorn. Heat the oil in a large, heavy-based, lidded saucepan, with a couple of kernels in the pan. Once you hear those pop, add the rest of the popcorn kernels to the pan and cover with a lid. Shake the pan now and again as the corn starts to pop and continue heating until the popping stops. Remove from the heat and spread the popcorn out on the prepared baking trays.

To make the caramel, put the sugar, syrup and 100 ml water in a saucepan and heat very gently, stirring occasionally, until the sugar has dissolved. Bring to the boil and, without stirring, heat to 140ºC (275ºF). (If you don't have a sugar thermometer, drop a little of the syrup into a glass of chilled water. When cool, you should be able to pull it into firm, pliable threads.) Remove from the heat and carefully drizzle the syrup over the popcorn.

Leave to cool completely, then lift the popcorn off the baking trays with a metal spatula and break up any large chunks that have stuck together.

Store the popcorn in an airtight container until required. These can be made up to 4 days in advance.

toffee apples

10 well-flavoured apples,
such as braeburn or
pink lady

450 g golden caster sugar

50 g butter

4 tablespoons golden
syrup

*10 wooden lolly sticks
or short, slim dowels*

*a baking tray, lined with
non-stick baking paper*

makes 10

Lovely for an autumn wedding, these sweet apples have a wonderfully
nostalgic feel and look gorgeous wrapped in clear cellophane and tied
with coloured string and a decorative leaf. Tie on a gift tag from the bride
and groom or simply pop an apple in the centre of each place setting.

Wash the apples in warm, soapy water, then rinse well and pat dry. Push a lolly stick
or short length of dowel into each apple.

Put the sugar and 200 ml water into a heavy-based saucepan and warm over a gentle
heat, stirring occasionally, until the sugar has dissolved. Stir in the butter and syrup,
then bring to the boil and continue to boil (without stirring) until the mixture reaches
140°C (275°F). (If you don't have a sugar thermometer, drop a little of the syrup into
a glass of chilled water. When cool, you should be able to pull it into firm, pliable
threads.) Remove the saucepan from the heat and quickly but carefully, dip each
apple in the toffee, turning until well coated. Leave to set on the prepared baking tray.

When completely set, store the apples in an airtight container until required. These
can be made up to 2 days in advance.

elderflower cordial

Sharp, sweet and tongue-tinglingly fragrant, this pretty pale pink
cordial makes the perfect gift for your guests to take away and
enjoy with sparkling water. Depending on the time of year you plan
to get married, bear in mind that this recipe freezes well, so you can
always make the cordial when elderflowers are in season and freeze
it until the wedding day. Choose flower heads with creamy white
open petals that are not yet beginning to drop.

900 g granulated sugar

2.5 litres boiling water

pink food colouring

1 packet citric acid (available
from chemists)

30 elderflower heads

2 thinly sliced lemons

*small sterilized bottles
(see page 4)*

makes about 2 litres

Put the sugar in a large heatproof bowl and pour over the boiling water. Add
a few drops of food colouring to make a delicate pink cordial and stir until the
sugar has dissolved. Set aside to cool.

Stir the citric acid into the cooled mixture. Gently rinse the flower heads then
add to the sugar syrup along with the lemons. Leave to stand for 24 hours,
stirring occasionally.

Strain the mixture through a muslin and bottle in sterilized bottles.

index